creepy creatures

Published by Creative Education
P.O. Box 227, Mankato, Minnesota 56002
Creative Education is an imprint of
The Creative Company
www.thecreativecompany.us

Design and production by Ellen Huber
Production by Chelsey Luther
Art direction by Rita Marshall
Printed in the United States of America

Photographs by Alamy (Nigel Cattlin), Bigstock
(South12th), Dreamstime (3drenderings), Getty
Images (Visuals Unlimited, Inc./AlexWild),
iStockphoto (james allred, Evgeniy Ayupov, Eric
Isselée, Oktay Ortakcioglu, TommyIX), National
Geographic Stock (DAVID LIITTSCHWAGER),
Photo Researchers (Eye of Science/Science Source),
Shutterstock (BMJ, Patricia Hofmeester, Sebastian
Kaulitzki, Kondor83, Sergey Peterman, Tomislav
Pinter, stevenku), SuperStock (Gallo Images, Science
Picture Co/Science Faction)

Library of Congress Cataloging-in-Publication Data
Bodden, Valerie.
Mites / Valerie Bodden.
p. cm. — (Creepy creatures)
Summary: A basic introduction to mites, examining
where they live, how they grow, what they eat, and
the unique traits that help to define them, such as
their ability to live on animals and in dust.
Includes bibliographical references and index.
ISBN 978-1-60818-357-9
1. Mites—Juvenile literature. I. Title. II. Series:
Bodden, Valerie. Creepy creatures.
QL458.B63 2014
595.4'2—dc23   2013009754

First Edition
9 8 7 6 5 4 3 2 1

CONTENTS

mites

VALERIE BODDEN

CREATIVE 🍎 EDUCATION

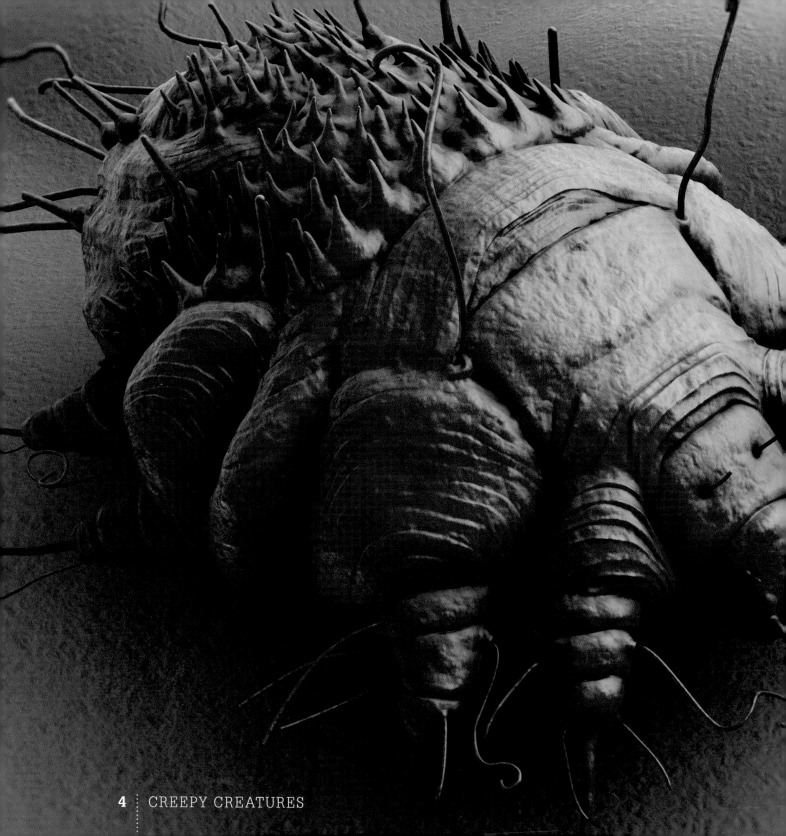

Sunlight shines onto a shelf in your house. You see dust. If you looked at the dust under a **microscope**, you might see something else. There could be lots of little creatures crawling around.

These are mites!

Mites are **arachnids** (*uh-RAK-nidz*). They belong to the same animal family as spiders. Mites have a circle-shaped body with eight legs.

Most mites cannot see, so they use other senses to find their way around

Many mites are brown, yellow, or red. Most are so small that you cannot see them without a microscope. But a few mites are as big as your thumbnail.

Mites can be so small that it is hard to know how many types there are

Some mites look like red dots, unless they are viewed close-up

Red velvet mites have two mouthparts that look like lobster claws

There can be 100,000 to 10 million dust mites living in a used mattress

There are about 30,000 kinds of mites. Dust mites live in dust. Follicle (*FOLL-ih-kuhl*) mites live on people's eyebrows and eyelashes. Red velvet mites live in dry and forested lands. They are red and fuzzy.

Some mites live in the ground or on plants. Others live in the sea. Some even live at the North and South Poles! Many mites live on other animals. Mites do not seem to have many **predators**. But some mites are eaten by bigger mites.

Some mites like to ride on the backs of beetles to get around

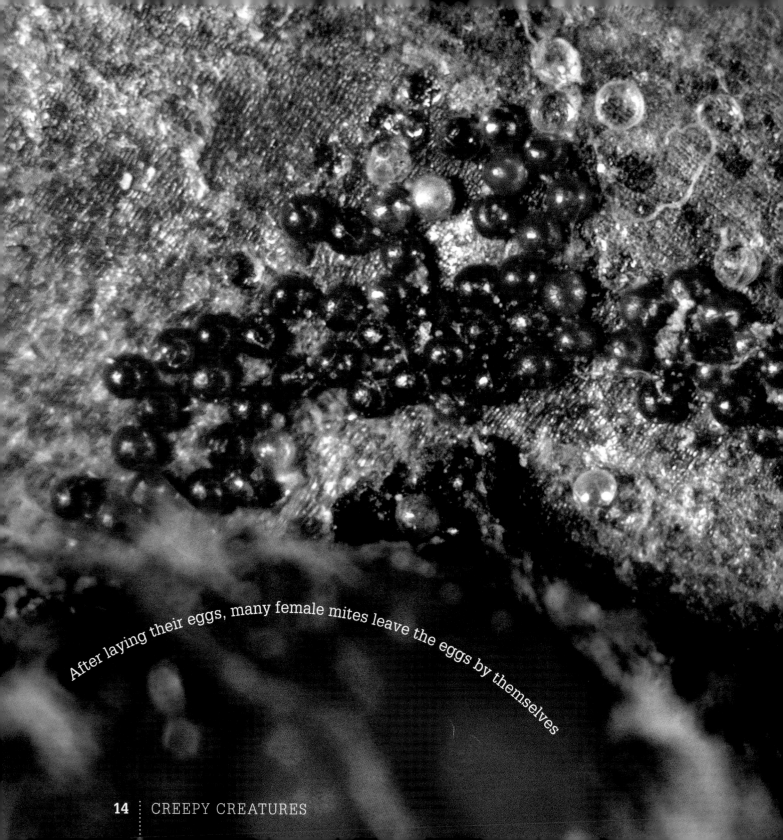

After laying their eggs, many female mites leave the eggs by themselves

Mites begin life in eggs. **Larvae** come out of the eggs. They have only six legs. When larvae become too big for their skin, they **molt**. Now they are **nymphs** (*NIMFS*). The nymphs molt, too. They become adults with eight legs. Most adult mites live for only a few weeks.

The dust mite (pictured) eats the dead skin that is found in dust

Some mites eat other animals'
blood. Other mites eat dead
skin from people and animals.
Many mites eat plants.

A leaf fed on by mites can change color and become bumpy

Mites can be helpful. Mites that eat dead skin keep it from piling up. Other mites eat and break down dead plants. This helps make good soil. But mites can bother people, too. Some people are **allergic** to dust mites. The scabies (*SKAY-bees*) mite can make people itch.

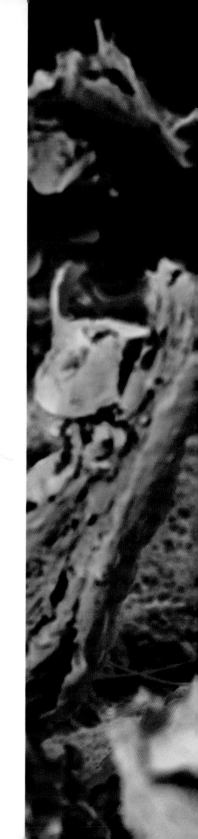

The scabies mite lives and lays it eggs on the upper layer of human skin

House dust mites do not live as long on hard surfaces that can be vacuumed easily

People sometimes use the word "mite" about things that are small. Some people call kids mites. A long time ago, a small coin was called a mite. We cannot see most mites, but it can be fun to learn about these tiny creepy creatures!

Mites were small coins made of copper more than 400 years ago

MAKE A MITE

You can make your own mite with two paper plates. Paint the bottom of both plates black. Cut eight thin rectangles from a piece of black paper for legs. Glue the legs around the outside of one of the paper plates. Place the second paper plate on top of the first plate so that the black side of each is showing. Glue the plates together to finish your mite!

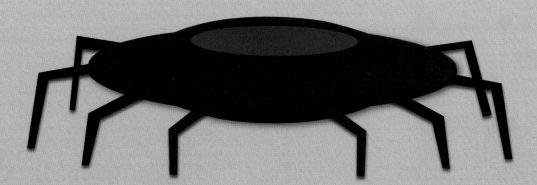

GLOSSARY

allergic: relating to the body's response to something such as dust or mold by sneezing, coughing, or itching

arachnids: small, eight-legged animals like spiders and ticks

larvae: the form some insects and animals take when they hatch from eggs, before changing into their adult form

microscope: a machine with special lenses that makes it possible to see very small things

molt: to lose a shell or layer of skin and grow a new, larger one

nymphs: young mites with eight legs

predators: animals that kill and eat other animals

READ MORE

Backyard. North Mankato, Minn.: Brown Bear Books, 2008.

Ward, Brian R. *Microscopic Life in the Home.* North Mankato, Minn.: Smart Apple Media, 2005.

WEBSITES

Mites and Ticks: A Virtual Introduction
http://www.sel.barc.usda.gov/acari/index.html
See close-up pictures of many kinds of mites.

PestWorld for Kids: Dust Mites
http://dev.pestworldforkids.org/dust-mites.html
Learn more about dust mites.

INDEX